Guide to Tailwind CSS

Practical Guide

A. De Quattro

Copyright © 2024

Guide to Tailwind CSS

1.Introduction

Tailwind CSS is a utility-first framework for creating web designs that is gaining popularity in the front-end developer community. It was created by Adam Wathan, Steve Schoger, and Jonathan Reinink as an alternative to traditional CSS frameworks like Bootstrap and Foundation.

The approach of Tailwind CSS is unique, as it is based on a set of atomic CSS classes that can be used to build virtually any style without the need to write custom CSS. This approach has proven to be extremely flexible and powerful, allowing developers to create highly customized and responsive designs quickly and efficiently.

One of the distinctive features of Tailwind CSS is its "utility-first" approach. This means that instead of writing many custom CSS rules, you can use the classes provided by the framework to apply styles directly in the

HTML. For example, instead of having to write custom CSS to add margin to an element, you can simply use the class "mt-4" to add a top margin of 4 units.

In addition to classes for margins and padding, Tailwind CSS provides a wide range of utilities for managing colors, typography, alignments, sizes, backgrounds, borders, and much more. This allows developers to create complex and detailed styles without having to write custom CSS for each individual component.

Another key feature of Tailwind CSS is its configurability. The framework provides a configuration file that allows developers to customize the available classes, modify default colors, add new utilities, and much more. This makes Tailwind CSS extremely flexible and adaptable to the specific needs of each project.

Furthermore, Tailwind CSS is highly

performant thanks to its approach of generating classes only for the utilities actually used in the final project. This means that even though the framework provides a wide range of utilities, only those actually used will be included in the final CSS bundle, reducing file size and improving site performance.

Tailwind CSS is a groundbreaking CSS framework that stands out from the traditional frameworks we are accustomed to. Created by Adam Wathan, it is based on a completely different approach to creating web interfaces, offering all the basic elements needed to design without having to fight against predefined styles.

Traditional frameworks, like Bootstrap, offer a set of predefined components such as buttons, cards, modals, and forms, which can certainly speed up the design and prototyping process. However, they become limiting when it comes to customizing the design. Tailwind CSS breaks these limitations by providing utility classes that allow you to create exactly what you have in mind, without constantly having to abandon HTML.

Despite its young age, the first stable version of Tailwind CSS, version 1.0, was released in May 2019 and has since gained considerable success. The framework has attracted the interest of the front-end developer community, becoming one of the favorite and most satisfying to use according to the survey conducted by The State of CSS.

One of the distinctive features of Tailwind CSS is its ability to create responsive and mobile-oriented designs. Each utility class provides responsive variants that allow you to adapt behavior based on screen sizes. Responsive variants use intuitive prefixes like {screen}: to facilitate use and understanding.

Furthermore, Tailwind CSS supports the creation of components to avoid constant repetition of classes. You can define components that group together a set of specific classes, making it easier to manage code and maintain it.

Another strength of Tailwind CSS is its extreme customization. Thanks to configuration-based generation using JavaScript and PostCSS, you can modify every aspect of the framework directly during compilation, without the need to override existing styles or use !important directives within style sheets.

In the upcoming lessons, we will explore more deeply the features and capabilities of Tailwind CSS, revealing how it can be a valid alternative to traditional CSS frameworks.

Finally, Tailwind CSS is well supported by an active community of developers who provide plugins, tools, and useful resources to extend the framework's functionality and streamline the development process. Additionally, the Tailwind CSS development team is constantly working to improve and update the framework to ensure the highest quality and best possible performance.

Tailwind CSS is an innovative and powerful CSS framework that offers a unique approach to web design. With its wide range of utilities, configurability, and optimal performance, Tailwind CSS is quickly becoming one of the preferred frameworks among the front-end developer community. If you are looking for an efficient and flexible way to create customized and responsive web designs, Tailwind CSS may be the ideal choice for you.

2.Installation of Tailwind CSS

Thanks to its utility-first approach, Tailwind CSS provides a complete set of predefined CSS classes that cover virtually every aspect of a website's style, allowing you to design efficiently and modularly.

Installing Tailwind CSS is quite simple and can be done in a few steps. In this tutorial, we will guide you through the process of installing Tailwind CSS following the method recommended by the development team.

Before getting started, it is important to ensure that you have Node.js installed on your computer. Node.js is a server-side JavaScript execution environment that allows you to use npm (Node Package Manager) to manage dependencies for JavaScript projects.

Step 1: Create a new project

The first step to install Tailwind CSS is to create a new Node.js project and npm. You can do this by running the following command in a new folder:

```
npm init -y
```

This command will create a `package.json` file in your project folder with the default configuration. Next, you will need to install Tailwind CSS, PostCSS, and autoprefixer as project dependencies.

Step 2: Install Tailwind CSS, PostCSS, and autoprefixer

To install Tailwind CSS, PostCSS, and autoprefixer, run the following commands:

```
npm install tailwindcss postcss autoprefixer
```

Additionally, you will need to create a PostCSS configuration file called `postcss.config.js` in your project folder and add the following code to it:

```js
module.exports = {
  plugins: [
    require('tailwindcss'),
    require('autoprefixer'),
  ]
}
```

This configuration tells PostCSS to use

Tailwind CSS and autoprefixer to process the CSS files in your project.

Step 3: Create a basic CSS file

After installing the necessary dependencies, you need to create a basic CSS file in which to include Tailwind CSS. You can do this by creating a new file called `styles.css` in your project folder and adding the following code:

```css
@tailwind base;
@tailwind components;
@tailwind utilities;
```

This code imports the basic utilities, components, and utility classes of Tailwind CSS into your project. You can now import this CSS file into your HTML project to use

Tailwind CSS in your pages.

Step 4: Compile the CSS file with PostCSS

Once you have created the basic CSS file, you need to compile the CSS file using PostCSS to process the Tailwind CSS classes. You can do this by running the following command:

```
npx postcss styles.css -o output.css
```

This command will process the `styles.css` file using PostCSS with the Tailwind CSS and autoprefixer configurations, and then generate a new `output.css` file containing the compiled CSS code.

Step 5: Link the compiled CSS file to your HTML project

Finally, link the compiled CSS file to your HTML project by adding a line in the `<head>` tag of your HTML file:

```html
<link rel="stylesheet" href="output.css">
```

This way, your HTML project will be linked to the compiled CSS file containing the Tailwind CSS classes, allowing you to use Tailwind CSS utilities in your web pages.

With these steps, you have successfully installed Tailwind CSS in your Node.js project and are ready to start using this powerful CSS framework to design customizable and highly flexible web interfaces. Tailwind CSS offers an efficient and modular way to manage the style of your web pages, allowing you to easily create appealing and responsive designs.

3. Tailwind CSS Configuration

The configuration of Tailwind CSS is divided into three main steps: installation, customization, and integration.

To start using Tailwind CSS, you need to install the framework using npm or yarn. Once installed, you can customize colors, margins, padding, and many other properties in a dedicated file that will then be imported into the main configuration file.

One of the main advantages of Tailwind CSS is its ease of customization: you can create classes using the PostCSS preprocessor. Through a series of plugins, you can extend the framework with new features or customize existing classes. For example, you can add custom colors, modify margin or padding sizes, define new typography, and much more.

The `tailwind.config.js` file is the heart of

Tailwind CSS configuration. In this file, you can define all the configuration parameters of the framework. For example, you can set the main colors of the site, margin and padding sizes, default typography, and more. This file provides total control over how the framework should behave and what classes will be available to developers.

Another important aspect of Tailwind CSS configuration is the customization of themes. With themes, you can define sets of colors, typography, and other properties for different versions of the site. For example, you can create a light theme and a dark theme and allow users to choose which one to use. This offers further flexibility in site design and helps create a better user experience.

Once Tailwind CSS configuration and customization are complete, you need to integrate the framework into the front-end project. This can be done through various methods, such as including CSS directly in the HTML file or using a bundler like Webpack or Parcel. It is important to ensure that the CSS generated by Tailwind is optimized during the build process to ensure better performance.

One of the most interesting features of Tailwind CSS is its ability to be easily customized using CSS variables. This allows developers to easily create custom themes to fit their website design. Tailwind CSS CSS variables allow you to easily define colors, sizes, padding, margins, and many other CSS properties using a variable-based approach rather than predefined classes.

For example, if you want to change the primary color of the website, you can simply modify a CSS variable instead of having to manually search and replace all occurrences of the corresponding default class. This makes customizing website design much simpler and faster, allowing developers to focus more on the visual aspect of the website rather than on debugging and maintaining CSS code.

Additionally, Tailwind CSS also offers the ability to extend and configure your own set of custom CSS utilities. This allows developers to extend Tailwind's functionality by adding new classes and custom styles to adapt to their specific needs. For example, you can define new classes to handle different typography, backgrounds, or borders, creating a customized CSS utility set that perfectly reflects the website design.

Tailwind CSS also allows you to easily configure various aspects of the framework, such as padding sizes, default margins, base colors, default fonts, and much more. This allows developers to tailor Tailwind to their needs and design preferences, ensuring greater control over the appearance and behavior of the website.

Another interesting feature of Tailwind CSS is the ability to enable or disable certain modules or components of the framework based on project needs. For example, you can disable the layout module if you want to use another framework to manage the grid or disable the responsive design module if you prefer to use a different approach for managing website responsiveness.

Furthermore, Tailwind CSS offers the ability to define global themes that can easily be applied to the entire website. This allows you to define a basic and uniform style for the entire website, facilitating consistency and design cohesion. Global themes can include color settings, typography, spacing, borders, and many other CSS properties, allowing developers to easily create a consistent and professional look for the entire website.

Theme and configurability in Tailwind CSS are two powerful tools that allow developers to customize and optimize website design and functionality in a simple and effective way.

Thanks to CSS variables, module configuration, and global themes, you can create a unique and customized design that perfectly fits the project's needs. Tailwind CSS is therefore a valid choice for developers looking for a flexible, powerful, and highly customizable CSS framework for creating modern and up-to-date websites.

Finally, it is important to keep in mind that Tailwind CSS is a powerful tool but can also be complex to manage in large projects. It is essential to organize the configuration clearly and structured to avoid confusion and ensure easy maintenance over time.

Tailwind CSS configuration requires time and attention, but the benefits it offers in terms of development speed and design flexibility make it a very powerful tool for front-end developers. With proper configuration and class management, you can efficiently and cleanly create modern and responsive interfaces.

4. Using Tailwind utility classes

Tailwind CSS is a popular "utility-first" CSS framework that allows developers to create a highly customized design system without writing CSS code. One of the main features of Tailwind CSS is its extensive collection of utility classes, which can be used to style various elements on a website.

In this article, we will explore how to use the utility classes provided by Tailwind CSS to style different elements and components in a web application.

Basic Utility Classes

Tailwind CSS provides a wide range of utility classes that can be used to style different properties of an element. These utility classes are organized into categories such as spacing, typography, colors, and more.

One of the most commonly used utility classes in Tailwind CSS is the `bg-{color}` class, which can be used to apply a background color to an element. For example, to apply a blue background color to a div element, you can use the `bg-blue-500` class.

```html
<div class="bg-blue-500">
  This is a blue div
</div>
```

Another useful utility class is `text-{color}`, which can be used to apply a text color to an element. For example, to apply a red text color to a paragraph element, you can use the `text-red-500` class.

```html
<p class="text-red-500">
```

This is a red paragraph

</p>

```

## Spacing Utility Classes

Tailwind CSS provides a series of utility classes that can be used to adjust the margins and padding of an element. These classes are named based on the property they modify, such as margin, padding, and space.

For example, you can use the `p-4` class to apply a padding of 1rem on all sides of an element. Similarly, you can use the `m-2` class to apply a margin of 0.5rem on all sides of an element.

```html
<div class="p-4 m-2">
  This is a div with padding and margin

```
</div>
```

You can also use directional classes to apply different margins and padding to individual sides of an element. For example, you can use the `mt-2` class to apply a margin of 0.5rem on the top of an element.

```html
<div class="mt-2">
  This is a div with top margin
</div>
```

Responsive Utility Classes

Tailwind CSS provides responsive utility classes that allow you to apply different styles based on the screen size. These classes are prefixed with `sm:`, `md:`, `lg:`, and `xl:` to target small, medium, large, and extra-large screens respectively.

For example, you can use the `sm:text-lg` class to apply a larger text size on small and up screens.

```html
<p class="text-sm md:text-lg">

  This text will be smaller on small screens and larger on medium and up screens

</p>
```

You can also combine multiple responsive classes to create complex styles that adapt to different screen sizes. For example, you can use the `md:flex lg:flex-row` class to change the flex direction of an element on medium and up screens.

```html
<div class="flex flex-col md:flex lg:flex-row">
  <!-- This element will be a column on small screens and a row on medium and up screens -->
</div>
```

Customizing Utility Classes

Tailwind CSS allows you to customize the utility classes provided by the framework to fit your web application's design system. You can do this by modifying the `tailwind.config.js` file in your project and adding or modifying utility classes in the `theme` section.

For example, it is possible to add a new custom color palette to Tailwind CSS by defining new colors in the `colors` object of the `theme` section.

```javascript
module.exports = {
  theme: {
    extend: {
      colors: {
        custom-blue: '#1E40AF',
        custom-red: '#DC2626',
      },
    },
  },
}
```

After customizing the utility classes, you can

use them in your HTML markup just like the default utility classes provided by Tailwind CSS.

``` html

<div class="bg-custom-blue text-custom-red">

  This is a div with custom background color and custom text color

</div>
```

Conclusion

In this article, we have explored how to use the utility classes provided by Tailwind CSS to style various elements and components in a web application. By leveraging the extensive collection of utility classes offered by Tailwind CSS, developers can create highly customized designs without having to write any CSS code.

From basic styling properties to responsive designs, Tailwind CSS utility classes provide a robust set of tools to help developers build modern and visually appealing web applications. By customizing these utility classes, developers can tailor the design system to meet the specific needs of their project and create a unique user experience for their audience.

5.Creating layouts with Tailwind

Learn how to create a layout using Tailwind CSS, providing detailed examples and explanations on how to use classes to define the structure of the page.

Before we begin, make sure you have installed Tailwind CSS in your project. You can do this via npm or yarn, by running the following command:

```
npm install tailwindcss
```

Once Tailwind CSS is installed, you can start creating your layout. Let's start by defining a basic structure for our web page.

```html
```

```html
<!DOCTYPE html>
<html lang="en">
<head>
    <meta charset="UTF-8">
    <meta name="viewport" content="width=device-width, initial-scale=1.0">
    <title>Layout with Tailwind</title>
    <link href="https://cdn.jsdelivr.net/npm/tailwindcss@2.2.19/dist/tailwind.min.css" rel="stylesheet">
</head>
<body class="bg-gray-100">
    <div class="container mx-auto">
        <header class="bg-blue-500 p-4 text-white">
            <h1 class="text-2xl font-bold">Header</h1>
        </header>
```

```html
<main class="p-4">
    <h2 class="text-xl font-bold">Main Content</h2>
    <p>Lorem ipsum dolor sit amet, consectetur adipiscing elit. Sed fringilla justo ac quam fringilla, ut blandit nisi fringilla. Cras vestibulum a eros sit amet commodo. Quisque at tristique erat. Nulla arcu est, bibendum in sapien nec, varius volutpat turpis. Nam semper ligula sit amet arcu varius varius. Fusce ut risus sem. Duis sed fe)ugiat ipsum. Aliquam in libero ac libero porta scelerisque. Integer blandit, arcu non placerat tincidunt, urna massa porttitor lectus, sed ultricies metus lacus id ante.</p>
</main>
<footer class="bg-gray-700 p-4 text-white text-center">
    Footer
</footer>
    </div>
</body>
</html>
```

```

In this example, we've defined a basic structure for our web page with a header, main content, and a footer. Using Tailwind CSS classes, we added colored backgrounds, padding, and text colors to define the style of different elements.

The "container mx-auto" class was used to center the content of the page and limit the maximum width of the content. The "p-4" classes were used to add padding to the header, main content, and footer.

For the header, we used the "bg-blue-500" class to set a blue background and the "text-white" class to set the text color to white. We also used the "p-4" classes to add space around the header content and "text-2xl font-bold" to define the title style.
```

For the main content, we used the "p-4" class to add padding around the content and the "text-xl font-bold" classes to define the title style. We also added a sample text paragraph using the "text-base" class.

Finally, for the footer, we used the "bg-gray-700" class to set a dark gray background and the "p-4 text-white text-center" classes to define the footer content style.

By using Tailwind CSS classes, you can easily customize the style and structure of the web page without the need for writing custom CSS. Tailwind CSS offers a wide range of predefined classes for layout management, colors, text types, and much more, making the creation of responsive layouts quick and efficient.

6. Responsiveness with Tailwind CSS

Tailwind CSS is a CSS framework that allows you to create responsive interfaces easily and quickly. Its philosophy is based on using utility classes to define styles directly within the markup, making it easier to create flexible layouts that adapt to different devices.

In this article, we will explore how to manage responsiveness with Tailwind CSS, using its utilities to create a design that optimally adjusts to screens of different sizes.

1. Predefined breakpoints

Tailwind CSS offers a set of predefined breakpoints that allow you to define different styles based on the device's width. The predefined breakpoints are:

- sm: from 0 to 640px

- md: from 641px to 768px

- lg: from 769px to 1024px

- xl: from 1025px onwards

To apply a specific style to a particular breakpoint, you can use the following classes:

- sm:sm-{property}-{value}

- md:md-{property}-{value}

- lg:lg-{property}-{value}

- xl:xl-{property}-{value}

For example, if you want to apply a different margin to an element depending on the device's width, you can use the following classes:

```html
<div class="mx-4 sm:mx-8 md:mx-16 lg:mx-32 xl:mx-64">Content</div>
```

```

This way, the element's margin will be 4 units by default, but will progressively increase as the device's width increases.

2. Hiding and showing elements

To manage the visibility of elements based on the device's width, Tailwind CSS offers the following utilities:

- hidden: hides an element
- block: shows an element
- inline: shows an element as inline
- inline-block: shows an element as inline-block
- flex: shows an element as a flex item
- grid: shows an element as a grid item
```

To hide an element on certain breakpoints, you can use the following classes:

- sm:hidden

- md:hidden

- lg:hidden

- xl:hidden

For example, if you want to hide an element on small devices, you can use the following class:

```html
<div class="hidden sm:block">Content visible only on small devices</div>
```

This way, the element will only be visible on screens larger than 640px.

3. Renaming classes

In Tailwind CSS, you can rename the predefined utility classes, allowing you to further customize the design based on your needs. To rename a class, you can use the `addUtilities` method within the `tailwind.config.js` configuration file.

For example, if you want to rename the class `lg:text-center` to `large:text-center`, you can add the following configuration to the `tailwind.config.js` file:

```javascript
module.exports = {
  theme: {
    extend: {},
  },
  plugins: [],
```

```
  corePlugins: {
    container: false,
  },
  utilities: {
    'large': 'lg',
  },
}
```

This way, the class `lg:text-center` can be used as `large:text-center`.

4. Customize breakpoints

If Tailwind CSS's default breakpoints do not meet your needs, you can customize them within the `tailwind.config.js` configuration file. To customize breakpoints, you can define the pixel sizes within the `screens` option.

For example, if you want to customize the breakpoints to suit the specific needs of your project, you can add the following configuration to the `tailwind.config.js` file:

```javascript
module.exports = {
  theme: {
    extend: {},
    screens: {
      'sm': '320px',
      'md': '640px',
      'lg': '1024px',
      'xl': '1280px',
    },
  },
  plugins: [],
  corePlugins: {
    container: false,
```

```
  },
}
```

This way, the breakpoints will be defined based on the sizes specified in the configuration file.

5. Customize classes

Tailwind CSS allows you to customize the default utility classes, allowing you to define new classes or overwrite existing ones. To customize classes, you can add your own configuration within the `tailwind.config.js` file.

For example, if you want to define new classes to handle the responsiveness of an element's width, you can add the following configuration to the `tailwind.config.js` file:

```javascript
module.exports = {
  theme: {
    extend: {
      width: {
        '1/10': '10%',
        '2/10': '20%',
        '3/10': '30%',
        '4/10': '40%',
        '5/10': '50%',
        '6/10': '60%',
        '7/10': '70%',
        '8/10': '80%',
        '9/10': '90%',
      },
    },
  },
```

```
  plugins: [],
  corePlugins: {
    container: false,
  },
}
```

This way, you can use the new classes to define the width of an element according to your needs.

Responsiveness with Tailwind CSS is extremely simple and efficient, thanks to the utilities provided by the framework. With just a few lines of code, you can create flexible layouts that adapt to different devices, improving the user experience on every screen. By leveraging the default and customized classes of Tailwind CSS, you can create modern and functional designs that perfectly fit the project's requirements.

7. Creating Components with Tailwind

In the world of web development, creating components is a fundamental part of the design and development process of a website or application. Tailwind CSS is a utility CSS framework that greatly simplifies the creation of responsive and customizable components. In this article, we will explore some examples of how to create different types of components using Tailwind.

Before starting to create components with Tailwind, it is important to understand some basic concepts of the framework. Tailwind is based on a series of utility classes that can be used directly in HTML markup to style elements. Tailwind classes can be combined to create complex styles, allowing for great flexibility in component design.

One of the main advantages of using Tailwind is its ease of use and effectiveness in creating responsive components. By using Tailwind's sizing and positioning classes, it is possible to create layouts that adapt to different screen sizes, ensuring a good user experience on devices of various formats.

An example of a component that we can create with Tailwind is a card element. Cards are containers that hold information or images and are very common in web application designs. To create a card element with Tailwind, we can use Tailwind classes to style the card and the elements inside it. Here is an example of how we could create a card element using Tailwind:

```html
<div class="bg-white shadow-md max-w-sm rounded-lg overflow-hidden">
  <img class="w-full" src="image.jpg" alt="image" />
  <div class="px-6 py-4">
    <div class="font-bold text-xl mb-2">Card Title</div>
```

```
    <p class="text-gray-700 text-base">
    Lorem ipsum dolor sit amet, consectetur adipiscing elit. Integer nec odio. Praesent libero.
    </p>
  </div>
</div>
```

In this example, we are creating a card element that contains an image, a title, and a description. We use Tailwind classes to set the background, shadow, rounded border of the card, and we included an image inside the card using the `w-full` class to make it expand to the full width of the card.

To format the content inside the card, we use Tailwind classes to set the padding and typography of the text. We use `px-6` and `py-4` to set horizontal and vertical padding respectively, and `font-bold` and `text-xl` to set the font weight and text size of the card title. Finally, we use `text-gray-700` and `text-base` to set the text color and text size of the description.

Another example of a component that we can create with Tailwind is a navbar. A navbar is a navigation bar that contains links to different sections of a website or application. Creating a navbar with Tailwind is very simple thanks to its sizing and positioning classes. Here is an example of how we could create a navbar using Tailwind:

```html
<nav class="bg-gray-800 p-6 flex justify-between items-center">
  <div class="text-white font-bold text-xl">Logo</div>
  <div>
    <a href="#" class="text-white hover:text-gray-300 px-4">Home</a>
    <a href="#" class="text-white hover:text-gray-300 px-4">Services</a>
```

```
    <a href="#" class="text-white hover:text-gray-300 px-4">Contact</a>
  </div>
</nav>
```

In this example, we are creating a navbar with a dark gray background and horizontal padding. We use the Tailwind classes `flex justify-between items-center` to align the contents of the navbar horizontally and vertically center the elements within the navbar.

Within the navbar, we have a text element with the site logo and three links to home, services, and contact. We use Tailwind classes to style the links, including hover styles to change the text color when hovered over with the mouse.

Another type of common component that we can create with Tailwind is a form element. Form elements are used to collect information from users, such as a registration form or a contact form. Creating a form element with Tailwind is very simple thanks to its pre-built input classes. Here is an example of how we could create a form element using Tailwind:

```html
<form class="bg-white shadow-md p-6">

  <label for="name" class="block text-gray-700 font-bold mb-2">Name</label>

  <input type="text" id="name" name="name" class="w-full p-2 border border-gray-300 rounded mb-4" />


  <label for="email" class="block text-gray-700 font-bold mb-2">Email</label>

  <input type="email" id="email" name="email" class="w-full p-2 border border-gray-300 rounded mb-4" />
```

```
    <button type="submit" class="bg-blue-500 hover:bg-blue-700 text-white font-bold py-2 px-4 rounded">
    Submit
    </button>
</form>
```

In this example, we are creating a form element with a white background and shadow. Inside the form, we have two input fields for name and email, both with a gray border and a padding of 2 units. We use Tailwind classes to set the style of the input fields and submit buttons, including hover styles to highlight them when the mouse is hovered over.

These are just a few examples of components we can create using Tailwind. With its wide range of utility classes, Tailwind allows us to easily create sophisticated and customizable components for our websites and web applications. We hope these examples have inspired you to further explore the potential of Tailwind in creating components and optimizing your frontend development workflow.

8. Extension of Tailwind CSS

One of the distinctive features of Tailwind CSS is the vast set of predefined utility classes that you can use to quickly style your design. However, you may find the need to create custom classes that are not available by default in the framework. To do this, you can extend Tailwind's utility classes by defining new classes in the `tailwind.config.js` configuration file.

For example, suppose you want to create a class that defines a dark blue background for your elements. You can add this custom class as follows:

```javascript
// tailwind.config.js

module.exports = {
  theme: {
```

```
    extend: {
      colors: {
        'dark-blue': '#2E4053',
      },
    },
  },
  variants: {},
  plugins: [],
}
```

Once you have defined the new class in the configuration file, you can use it in your HTML code:

```html
<div class="bg-dark-blue text-white p-4">
  This is text with a dark blue background
</div>
```

```

In this way, you have extended the default set of Tailwind CSS utility classes with a new `bg-dark-blue` class that defines a dark blue background for the element.

**Configuration of variants:**

Variants in Tailwind CSS allow you to define different styles for an element based on its states, such as `hover`, `focus`, `active`, etc. You can extend the default variants of Tailwind CSS or define new ones in the `tailwind.config.js` file.

For example, if you want to create a variant that changes the text color of an element when you hover over it, you can add it as follows:

```javascript

```js
// tailwind.config.js

module.exports = {
  theme: {},
  variants: {
    extend: {
      textColor: ['hover'],
    },
  },
  plugins: [],
}
```

This configuration extends the default set of Tailwind CSS variants by adding the `hover` variant to the `text-color` property. Now you can use this variant in your HTML code:

```html
```

```
<p class="text-blue-600 hover:text-blue-800">
  Hover here to change the text color
</p>
```

In this way, you have defined a new variant that changes the text color when you hover over the element.

Adding new utilities:

Tailwind CSS offers a comprehensive set of CSS utilities covering a wide range of styles and functionalities. However, you may have specific needs that require adding new utilities to the framework. You can do this by creating custom plugins and adding them to your project.

To add a new utility that defines an underlined

text style with a custom color, you can create a custom plugin in the `tailwind.config.js` file:

```javascript
// tailwind.config.js

const plugin = require('tailwindcss/plugin')

module.exports = {
  theme: {},
  variants: {},
  plugins: [
    plugin(function({ addUtilities, theme, e }) {
      const colors = theme('colors')

      const underlineColors = Object.keys(colors).reduce((acc, key) => {
        return {
          ...acc,
```

```
    [`.underline-${key}`]: {
      'text-decoration': 'underline',
      'text-decoration-color': colors[key],
    },
   }
  }, {})

  addUtilities(underlineColors)
 }),
],
}
```

In this example, the custom plugin defines a new utility that adds an underlined text style with a custom color for each color defined in the Tailwind CSS theme. Now you can use this new utility in your HTML code:

```html
<p class="underline-blue-600">
  This is underlined text with a blue color
</p>
```

In this way, you have extended the default set of Tailwind CSS utilities with a new utility that defines an underlined text style with a custom color.

Tailwind CSS offers excellent flexibility and extensibility that allows you to tailor the framework to the specific needs of your project. By using utility class extension, variant configuration, and adding new utilities, you can customize and enhance the design of your website with ease and precision. I hope this article has provided you with a useful overview of the extension capabilities of Tailwind CSS and inspired you to further explore its creative possibilities.

9.Customizing breakpoints

Tailwind CSS is a utility styling framework that offers a class-based approach to creating flexible and responsive designs. One of the most powerful features of Tailwind is the ability to customize breakpoints to fit the specific needs of a project.

Breakpoints are the points at which a website layout adapts to the screen size of the user's device. By default, Tailwind's predefined breakpoints are:

- `sm`: 640px

- `md`: 768px

- `lg`: 1024px

- `xl`: 1280px

However, it is possible to customize these breakpoints to fit the project's requirements.

To do so, you need to define the new breakpoints in the Tailwind configuration file, usually named `tailwind.config.js`.

Here is an example of how you can customize breakpoints in Tailwind CSS:

```javascript
// tailwind.config.js

module.exports = {
  theme: {
    screens: {
      'sm': '640px',
      'md': '768px',
      'lg': '1024px',
      'xl': '1280px',
      '2xl': '1536px',
    },
```

```
  },
}
```

In this example, I have added a new breakpoint called `'2xl'` with a width of 1536px. You can add as many breakpoint sizes as needed, depending on the project requirements.

Once you have defined the new breakpoints in the configuration file, you can use them in HTML markup by adding the corresponding Tailwind classes. For example, if you want a specific element to be hidden on screens with a `'2xl'` size and above, you can use the `hidden` class modified with the specific breakpoint:

```html
<div class="hidden 2xl:block">
  This text is only shown on 2xl screens and
```

above.

</div>

```

In this way, you can create flexible and responsive layouts using Tailwind CSS's customized breakpoints. This feature is particularly useful when working on projects that require designs adaptable to a wide range of devices and screen sizes.

In addition to customizing breakpoints, you can also define other options in the Tailwind configuration file, such as colors, typography, spacing, and more. Tailwind offers a wide range of styling utilities that can be easily customized to meet the specific needs of a project.

In conclusion, customizing breakpoints in Tailwind CSS allows you to create flexible and responsive designs that adapt to the screen size of the user's device. By using customized
```

breakpoints and Tailwind's utilities, you can create adaptable and optimized layouts for a variety of devices and screens, ensuring a consistent and high-quality user experience.

10. Mobile First

The concept of "Mobile First" is a design philosophy that emphasizes optimizing a website for mobile devices rather than desktop. This choice is driven by the increasing prevalence of smartphones and tablets for internet browsing, as well as the fact that search engines like Google now prioritize mobile-optimized sites.

When referring to "Mobile First," it means designing and developing a website starting from the mobile version and then adapting it for desktop, rather than the other way around as was common in the past. This approach ensures an optimal user experience on all devices, eliminating the risk of excessive complexity when transitioning from mobile to desktop.

To successfully implement a "Mobile First" design approach, it is essential to have a solid understanding of media queries and breakpoints. Breakpoints are specific points on which the responsive design of a website is based to adapt the layout and content to the screen size of the device. Breakpoints usually correspond to certain screen sizes, such as 768px for tablets and 1024px for desktops.

To customize breakpoints in a project using Tailwind CSS, you can use the "screens" constant within the tailwind.config.js configuration file. This allows you to define custom breakpoints and use them within the CSS code without manually inserting media queries.

For example, suppose you want to define two custom breakpoints to better manage the layout of a website. You can add these definitions to the "screens" constant inside tailwind.config.js like this:

```javascript
module.exports = {
  theme: {
    screens: {
      'sm': '640px',
      'md': '768px',
      'lg': '1024px',
      'xl': '1280px',
      '2xl': '1536px',
    }
  }
}
```

In this example, we have defined two new breakpoints, 'sm' and 'md', at 640px and 768px respectively. Now you can use these breakpoints within your CSS code using the corresponding classes in this way:

```html
<div class="text-center md:text-left lg:text-right">
  Lorem ipsum dolor sit amet.
</div>
```

In this case, the text will be centered on screens below 768px (sm), aligned left between 768px and 1024px (md), and aligned right on screens larger than 1024px (lg).

Tailwind CSS offers a wide range of CSS utilities that can be used to customize the website design quickly and easily. Using custom breakpoints and CSS utilities from Tailwind, you can create a responsive design suitable for all devices without the need for additional code for media queries.

The "Mobile First" approach is essential for ensuring an optimal user experience on mobile devices, while customizing breakpoints with Tailwind CSS allows you to create a responsive and adaptable design for different screens without writing additional CSS code. Using custom breakpoints and Tailwind CSS utilities, you can create a responsive and performant website quickly and easily.

11.Simple colors and palette of Tailwind CSS

Tailwind CSS is a popular CSS utility framework that allows you to easily create modern and responsive user interfaces. One of Tailwind's distinctive features is its simple and clean color palette, which allows you to design elegant and minimalist websites without having to write custom CSS. In this article, we will explore the simple colors and palette of Tailwind CSS, providing practical examples to help you use them in your project.

Basic color palette of Tailwind CSS

The basic color palette of Tailwind CSS includes a range of neutral and muted colors that serve as the foundation for your design. These colors can be used as backgrounds, text, borders, and more to create a consistent and professional look for your website.

Here are some examples of Tailwind CSS

basic colors:

- Light gray: #f7f7f7
- Medium gray: #e5e7eb
- Dark gray: #6b7280
- Black: #000000
- White: #ffffff

These colors can be easily used in your Tailwind projects by adding the appropriate classes to your HTML elements. For example, to assign a light gray background to an element, you can use the `bg-gray-100` class, while to change the text color to dark gray, you can use the `text-gray-700` class.

Theme color palette of Tailwind CSS

In addition to the basic colors, Tailwind CSS also includes a range of theme colors that can be used to add a touch of vitality to your design. These colors are divided into four groups: primary colors, alert colors, success colors, and error colors.

Here are some examples of Tailwind CSS theme colors:

Primary colors:

- Blue: #2b6cb0

- Green: #2f855a

- Red: #e53e3e

- Purple: #9333ea

Alert colors:

- Orange: #dd6b20

- Yellow: #d69e2e

Success colors:

- Dark green: #22543d

- Light green: #2b8448

Error colors:

- Dark red: #742a2a

- Light red: #c53030

These colors can be used to highlight specific parts of your design, such as buttons, alerts, confirmation messages, and so on. For example, you can use the `bg-blue-500` class to create a blue button or `bg-red-500` to highlight an error message.

Practical examples

To give you an idea of how you can use the Tailwind CSS color palette in your projects, here are some practical examples:

1. Creating a contact form:

Imagine you need to create a contact form for your website and want to use Tailwind CSS theme colors to highlight required fields. You can use the red color (#e53e3e) for the text of required fields and the green color (#2f855a) for the submit button of the form.

```
<div>
  <label for="name" class="text-gray-700">Nome</label>
  <input type="text" id="name" class="w-full border border-gray-300 rounded-md">
</div>
<div>
  <label for="email" class="text-gray-700">Email</label>
  <input type="email" id="email" class="w-full border border-gray-300 rounded-md">
</div>
<div>
  <label for="message" class="text-gray-
```

700">Messaggio</label>

```
  <textarea id="message" class="w-full border border-gray-300 rounded-md"></textarea>
</div>
<div class="mt-4">
  <button class="bg-green-500 text-white py-2 px-4 rounded-md">Invia</button>
</div>
```

2. Creating a responsive table:

If you need to design a responsive table to display data within your website, you can use Tailwind CSS's basic color palette to ensure that the table is easy to read and aesthetically pleasing.

```html
<div class="overflow-x-auto">
  <table class="w-full table-auto">
    <thead>
      <tr>
        <th class="text-left">Nome</th>
        <th class="text-left">Email</th>
        <th class="text-left">Ruolo</th>
      </tr>
    </thead>
    <tbody>
      <tr>
```

```html
        <td class="border px-4 py-2">John Doe</td>
        <td class="border px-4 py-2">john.doe@example.com</td>
        <td class="border px-4 py-2">Amministratore</td>
      </tr>
      <tr>
        <td class="border px-4 py-2">Jane Smith</td>
        <td class="border px-4 py-2">jane.smith@example.com</td>
        <td class="border px-4 py-2">Utente</td>
      </tr>
    </tbody>
  </table>
</div>
```

In this example, we have used Tailwind CSS's basic colors to ensure that the table is well-structured and easily readable on devices of various sizes.

Tailwind CSS's simple and clean color palette offers a wide range of options for designing modern and responsive user interfaces. By using Tailwind's basic and themed colors, you can create a consistent and professional design for your website without having to write custom CSS.

12. Extending the framework: Tailwind CSS plugins

Tailwind CSS is a utility-first framework that offers a wide range of predefined CSS classes for designing and styling a website. However, there may be cases where you want to add custom functionality or components to the Tailwind library to tailor it to your specific needs. In these cases, you can extend the framework using Tailwind CSS plugins.

Tailwind CSS plugins allow developers to extend the set of default classes with new custom features. This provides the flexibility to adapt the framework to the project's needs without the need to write additional CSS or override existing classes.

To start using Tailwind CSS plugins, you first need to install and configure Tailwind in the project. Once that is done, you can add and configure plugins to add custom functionality to the framework.

An example of a Tailwind CSS plugin could be a plugin for creating custom themes. This plugin could provide a set of classes to easily modify the colors, fonts, and other design attributes of the website without having to write custom CSS. For example, it could offer classes like `.theme-primary`, `.theme-secondary`, `.theme-accent`, which allow you to quickly apply different color combinations to the website design.

To create a Tailwind CSS plugin, you need to define an array of CSS utilities within a JavaScript file. The utilities should be defined as objects with a specific structure that includes the class name, CSS property values, and any variants or modifiers. For example:

```javascript
module.exports = {
  theme: {
    extend: {
```

```
    colors: {
      'primary': '#FF6347',
      'secondary': '#3A86FF',
      'accent': '#FFD700',
    },
   }
  }
 }
```

Once the plugin is defined, you can import it into the Tailwind CSS configuration file and use it in the project. This will allow you to use the new classes defined in the plugin to customize the website's style.

Another example of a Tailwind CSS plugin could be a plugin for creating custom UI components. This type of plugin could provide classes for creating modals, dropdowns, tabs, and other interactive elements that can be easily integrated into the website. For example, it could offer classes like `.modal`, `.dropdown`, `.tabs`, which allow you to quickly and easily create these elements within the website design.

Furthermore, Tailwind CSS plugins allow you to create custom classes for managing site responsiveness. For example, plugins could be defined for creating classes to manage the visibility of elements on different screen sizes, or for creating flexible layouts that adapt to screen sizes. This provides precise control over the layout and presentation of the site on desktop, tablet, and mobile devices.

Tailwind CSS plugins offer a wide range of possibilities for customizing and extending the framework based on the project's needs. Whether it's adding custom functionality, creating custom UI components, or managing site responsiveness, plugins offer the flexibility needed to adapt Tailwind CSS to specific requirements.

Tailwind CSS plugins are a powerful tool for extending and customizing the utility-first framework. By using plugins, you can add custom functionality, create custom UI components, and manage site responsiveness in a simple and effective way. With the flexibility offered by plugins, you can tailor Tailwind CSS to the specific needs of the project and create unique and custom designs without the need for additional CSS.

13. Useful Resources of Tailwind CSS

Tailwind CSS is a CSS framework that has quickly gained popularity among web developers for its flexibility and ease of use. It offers a wide range of useful resources that make it easy to create modern and responsive designs for websites and applications.

One of the key features of Tailwind CSS is its utility-first approach, which results in a large number of CSS classes that can be applied directly to HTML to define styles and layouts without the need to write custom CSS code. This methodology allows for quickly creating consistent and customizable designs while maintaining a good separation between structure and style.

Among the useful resources of Tailwind CSS, standout utility classes for positioning, sizing, and spacing of elements. For example, you can use classes like "m-4" to add margins of 4 units to an element, or "p-8" to set padding of

8 units. These classes make it easy to manage the layout of elements on the page without having to write additional CSS code.

Additionally, Tailwind CSS offers a wide range of utility classes for managing colors and backgrounds of elements. Classes like "bg-blue-500" allow for quickly setting the background color of an element using a predefined color scale, while classes like "text-white" allow for setting the text color. These classes facilitate design customization without having to manually define every single color in the stylesheet.

Another useful resource of Tailwind CSS is represented by the utility classes for managing typography. You can use classes like "text-xl" to quickly set the text size based on the framework's default typographic scale, or classes like "font-semibold" for bold or "italic" for italics. These classes simplify text style management in designs and help maintain visual consistency throughout the site.

Tailwind CSS also includes a series of plugins and predefined components that extend the framework's functionalities. For example, you can use the "forms" plugin to easily create HTML forms with predefined styles and formatting, or the "cards" plugin to quickly add design cards to pages. These plugins make it easy to create complex components without having to write custom CSS code.

Finally, Tailwind CSS offers extensive documentation and an active community of developers that provides support and additional resources. The documentation includes detailed examples of using utility classes, guides for integrating with various JavaScript frameworks and libraries, as well as tips for optimizing code performance and compatibility. The developer community also offers insights, advice, and useful resources to make the most of the framework's capabilities.

Example: To add a padding of 4 units to an HTML element using Tailwind, you can use the class "p-4" as shown below:

<div class="p-4">Content with 4-unit padding</div>

Tailwind Play: Tailwind Play is a fantastic online tool that allows you to quickly experiment with Tailwind CSS code and see the results in real-time. You can directly edit the classes in the editor and instantly see how they affect the appearance of the HTML element. This tool is extremely useful for testing new ideas and understanding how to combine Tailwind classes to achieve the desired result.

Example: In the Tailwind Play screen, you can input the following HTML code to create a button with a blue background and white text:

<button class="bg-blue-500 text-white p-

2">Click here</button>

Tailwind Toolbox: Tailwind Toolbox is a collection of components and templates built with Tailwind CSS that can be used as a starting point for web design. This resource offers a wide range of preset components such as headers, footers, cards, forms, and more, which can be easily customized and integrated into your projects. It's a great tool to save time during development and achieve a consistent and professional design.

Example: If you want to use a responsive navigation menu already designed with Tailwind CSS, you can copy the code from the example on Tailwind Toolbox and paste it directly into your project.

Tailwind CSS IntelliSense: Tailwind CSS IntelliSense is an extension for Visual Studio Code that provides automatic suggestions for Tailwind CSS classes as you type the code. This tool makes code writing faster and more efficient, as it allows quick access to available classes and displays detailed descriptions of each class while writing the code. It is particularly useful for those who want to learn to use Tailwind CSS more quickly and effectively.

Example: With Tailwind CSS IntelliSense extension activated in Visual Studio Code, you can start typing a class like "bg-" and all suggestions for background colors available in Tailwind CSS will be displayed, along with a brief description of each class.

Tailwind UI: Tailwind UI is a complete library of components and designs ready to be used with Tailwind CSS. This resource provides a wide range of well-designed components such as navigation menus, modals, tables, forms, and more, which can be easily integrated into your projects. Tailwind UI is a paid resource, but it can be a valuable investment for those who want to save time in design and achieve high-quality results.

Example: If you want to use a default modal from Tailwind UI, you can copy the code from the example on the platform and integrate it directly into your project to add a responsive and well-designed modal.

In conclusion, the useful resources of Tailwind CSS can help you improve your productivity, achieve high-quality design results, and learn to use this framework effectively. With the official documentation, Tailwind Play, Tailwind Toolbox, Tailwind CSS IntelliSense, and Tailwind UI at your disposal, you have all the necessary tools to develop responsive and customizable web projects with ease. Whether you are a beginner or an expert, these resources can be valuable in your learning and development journey with Tailwind CSS.

The useful resources of Tailwind CSS are a fundamental element to make the most of this CSS framework. Thanks to utility classes, preset plugins, and detailed documentation, it is possible to quickly and efficiently create modern and responsive designs while maintaining a good separation between structure and style. Tailwind CSS continues to be an ideal choice for web developers who want a flexible and powerful framework for creating quality websites and applications.

14. Tailwind CSS Glossary

The Tailwind CSS Glossary lists and explains the most common classes within the framework, providing practical examples to illustrate their usage.

1. Layout:

- Container:

The "container" class defines a container with a fixed width and is horizontally centered on the page. It is useful for limiting the width of content and making it more readable on large screens.

Example: <div class="container">...</div>

- Grid:

Tailwind CSS offers classes for creating grid layouts. Classes like "grid", "grid-cols-2", and "gap-4" allow for easy definition of grid structure and column spacing.

Example: `<div class="grid grid-cols-2 gap-4">...</div>`

2. Typography:

- Text:

The "text-xs", "text-sm", "text-base", "text-lg", and "text-xl" classes set the text size to extra-small, small, base, large, and extra-large respectively. These classes make it easy to manage text size within a project.

Example: `<p class="text-lg">Lorem ipsum dolor sit amet</p>`

- Font:

With Tailwind CSS's predefined font classes, you can customize the font-family used in the project. Classes like "font-sans", "font-serif", and "font-mono" allow for quick setting of the desired font style.

Example: `<p class="font-serif">Lorem ipsum dolor sit amet</p>`

3. Colors:

- Background:

Classes like "bg-red-500", "bg-blue-300", and "bg-green-700" easily set the background color of an HTML element. You can use a wide range of predefined colors in the framework or customize them as needed.

Example: <div class="bg-blue-500">...</div>

- Text:

To manage text color within a project, you can use classes like "text-red-500", "text-gray-800", "text-green-600", and so on. These classes allow for easy customization of text color based on design needs.

Example: <p class="text-gray-800">Lorem ipsum dolor sit amet</p>

4. Spacing:

- Margin:

Tailwind CSS margin classes easily define

space around HTML elements. Classes like "m-4", "mt-8", "mr-12" set margins of varying sizes in specified directions.

Example: <div class="m-4">...</div>

- Padding:

Similar to margin classes, padding classes like "p-4", "pt-8", "pr-12" set the internal space of HTML elements. You can easily customize internal space based on design needs.

Example: <div class="p-4">...</div>

5. Border:

- Border:

Tailwind CSS offers a wide range of classes to manage borders of HTML elements. Classes like "border", "border-2", "border-solid", "border-gray-300" easily define border style, thickness, and color.

Example: <div class="border border-2 border-gray-300">...</div>

- Rounded:

To round the corners of HTML elements, you can use classes like "rounded-sm", "rounded-md", "rounded-lg", "rounded-xl". These classes easily define the degree of corner rounding.

Example: <div class="rounded-lg">...</div>

6. Interactivity:

- Hover:

Tailwind CSS hover classes define specific styles to be applied when the cursor hovers over an element. For example, the class "hover:bg-gray-200" will change the background color of the element on cursor hover.

Example: <button class="hover:bg-gray-200">Click here</button>

- Transition:

To add a transition effect to an HTML element, you can use classes like "transition-all", "transition-colors", "transition-opacity". These classes specify the desired duration and type of transition.

Example: <div class="transition-all duration-300">...</div>

7. Utility:

- Invisible:

The "invisible" class defines an HTML element as invisible but retains the space it occupies on the page structure. This class can be used to temporarily hide elements without altering the layout.

Example: <div class="invisible">...</div>

- Overflow:

To manage overflow of HTML elements, you can use classes like "overflow-hidden", "overflow-auto", "overflow-scroll". These classes easily handle horizontal and vertical overflow of elements.

Example: `<div class="overflow-scroll">...</div>`

The Tailwind CSS Glossary provides a comprehensive overview of the utility classes offered by the framework, illustrating the usage of each with practical examples. By using Tailwind CSS's predefined classes, you can efficiently and quickly create custom designs, reducing the need for writing custom CSS. By leveraging the capabilities of Tailwind CSS, you can develop elegant and modern projects with ease.

15. Examples of Tailwind Applications

Tailwind CSS is a utility CSS framework that allows for easily creating responsive and customizable designs for websites. Thanks to its numerous useful classes, it is possible to create layouts and styles without the need to write new custom CSS. In this article, we will explore some examples of Tailwind CSS applications and how to use it to create website designs.

Example 1: Creating a Navigation Bar

One of the first things often created when designing a website is the navigation bar. Using Tailwind CSS, it is possible to easily create a responsive and customizable navigation bar. Below is an example code for creating a simple navigation bar with Tailwind CSS:

```html
```

```html
<nav class="bg-gray-800 p-4">
  <div class="container mx-auto flex justify-between items-center">
    <a href="#" class="text-white font-bold">Logo</a>
    <ul class="flex space-x-4">
      <li><a href="#" class="text-white">Home</a></li>
      <li><a href="#" class="text-white">About</a></li>
      <li><a href="#" class="text-white">Contact</a></li>
    </ul>
  </div>
</nav>
```

In this code, we are using Tailwind CSS classes to set the dark gray background (`bg-gray-800`), padding (`p-4`), auto margin (`mx-auto`), content flexing (`flex`), center alignment of elements (`justify-between`, `items-center`), spacing between elements (`space-x-4`), and text color (`text-white`).

This example demonstrates how Tailwind CSS can make it simple to create a navigation bar with a clean and modern design.

Example 2: Creating a Product Grid

Another common use of Tailwind CSS is creating grids of products or elements on a web page. Below is an example code for creating a product grid with Tailwind CSS:

```html
<div class="container mx-auto grid grid-cols-1 md:grid-cols-3 gap-4">
  <div class="bg-white p-4">
    <img src="image1.jpg" alt="Product 1" class="w-full">
    <h3 class="text-lg font-bold mt-2">Product 1</h3>
    <p class="text-gray-600">Description of Product 1</p>
    <button class="bg-blue-500 text-white px-4 py-2 mt-2">Buy Now</button>
  </div>
  <div class="bg-white p-4">
```

```html
    <img src="image2.jpg" alt="Product 2" class="w-full">
    <h3 class="text-lg font-bold mt-2">Product 2</h3>
    <p class="text-gray-600">Description of Product 2</p>
    <button class="bg-blue-500 text-white px-4 py-2 mt-2">Buy Now</button>
  </div>
  <div class="bg-white p-4">
    <img src="image3.jpg" alt="Product 3" class="w-full">
    <h3 class="text-lg font-bold mt-2">Product 3</h3>
    <p class="text-gray-600">Description of Product 3</p>
    <button class="bg-blue-500 text-white px-4 py-2 mt-2">Buy Now</button>
  </div>
</div>
```

In this example, we are using Tailwind CSS classes to set the maximum width of the container (`container`), auto margin (`mx-auto`), padding (`p-4`), bottom margin (`mb-4`), layout grid with one column on mobile display and 3 columns on desktop (`grid grid-cols-1 md:grid-cols-3`), spacing between elements (`gap-4`), white background (`bg-white`), image resizing (`w-full`), bold text (`font-bold`), gray text color (`text-gray-600`), and background and text color of the button (`bg-blue-500`, `text-white`).

This example shows how to use Tailwind CSS to easily create a product grid with a clean and responsive design.

Example 3: Creating a Contact Form

Finally, another common application of Tailwind CSS is creating contact forms or other input forms on a web page. Below is an example code for creating a contact form with Tailwind CSS:

```html
<form class="w-full max-w-lg mx-auto p-4">
  <div class="mb-4">
    <label for="name" class="block text-sm font-bold">Name</label>
    <input type="text" id="name" name="name" class="w-full px-3 py-2 border rounded-lg">
  </div>
  <div class="mb-4">
    <label for="email" class="block text-sm font-bold">Email</label>
    <input type="email" id="email"
```

```
    name="email" class="w-full px-3 py-2 border rounded-lg">
  </div>
  <div class="mb-4">
    <label for="message" class="block text-sm font-bold">Message</label>
    <textarea id="message" name="message" class="w-full px-3 py-2 border rounded-lg"></textarea>
  </div>
  <button type="submit" class="bg-blue-500 text-white px-4 py-2">Send</button>
</form>
```

In this example, we are using Tailwind CSS classes to set the maximum width of the form (`w-full max-w-lg`), auto margin (`mx-auto`), padding (`p-4`), bottom margin (`mb-4`), right and left margin (`px-3`), top and bottom margin (`py-2`), rounded border (`rounded-lg`), background and text color of the button (`bg-blue-500`, `text-white`), and labels (`block text-sm font-bold`) for input fields.

This example illustrates how Tailwind CSS can be used to easily create a contact form with a clean and simple design.

Tailwind CSS is a powerful CSS framework that allows for creating responsive and customizable designs in a simple and fast way. By using its numerous useful classes, it is possible to easily create a wide range of design elements for websites. The three examples above show how Tailwind CSS can be used to create a navigation bar, a product grid, and a contact form with ease and style. If you are looking for a simple way to create designs for your website, Tailwind CSS could be the solution for you.

Index

1. Introduzione pg.4

2. Installation of Tailwind CSS pg.10

3. Tailwind CSS Configuration pg.16

4. Using Tailwind utility classes pg.23

5. Creating layouts with Tailwind pg.32

6. Responsiveness with Tailwind CSS pg.37

7. Creating Components with Tailwind pg.47

8. Extension of Tailwind CSS pg.55

9. Customizing breakpoints pg.64

10. Mobile First pg.69

11. Simple colors and palette of Tailwind CSS pg.74

12. Extending the framework: Tailwind CSS plugins pg.83

13. Useful Resources of Tailwind CSS pg.88

14. Tailwind CSS Glossary pg.96

15. Examples of Tailwind Applications pg.103

www.ingramcontent.com/pod-product-compliance
Lightning Source LLC
Chambersburg PA
CBHW071937210526
45479CB00002B/716